# HELP, LORD!

# I'M RAISING
# A TEENAGER!

## E. L. Warren

insight *i* publishing group
Tulsa, Oklahoma

**Help, Lord! I'm Raising a Teenager!**

*Help, Lord! I'm Raising a Teenager!* by E. L. Warren
Published by Insight Publishing Group
8801 S. Yale, Suite 410
Tulsa, OK 74137
918-493-1718

Unless otherwise noted, all Scripture quotations are from the King James Version of the Bible.

Cover design by: Ed McConnell

ISBN 1-930027-38-9
Library of Congress catalog card number: 2001089517

*Printed in the United States of America*

# *DEDICATION*

I dedicate this book to the parents of teenagers and soon-to-be teenagers. If you feel overwhelmed or challenged, here's a little encouragement. I also dedicate this book to the teenagers who will eventually become parents. This book will show you how to sow a solid future for you and your teenagers to come. Help is here!

# *ACKNOWLEDGMENTS*

First, I want to thank God for the gift of the Holy Ghost and for His illumination of the Word of God, which allows us to produce practical presentations of His promises. Second, I say thank you to Ella, my wife, my princess of twenty-three years, who gave me these three treasures called teenagers. And thank you to my teens—Valecia, Malessa, and Rod—for being the vessels that endured the hardships of wrong decisions and for becoming the kingdom specimens for this work.

A final thanks to Pam Markert, my editorial assistant, for the countless hours devoted to this labor of love, and to a donor (who desires to remain anonymous) who made the financial part of this project a reality.

# _ENDORSEMENTS_

_Help, Lord! I'm Raising a Teenager!_ is very insightful and well written. It is the perspective of a pastor and a parent, and that spells experience. It should be mandatory reading for every teenager and parent before any relational crisis.

Dr. Kirby Clements
Bishop, Cathedral at Chapel Hill
Decatur, Georgia

_Help, Lord! I'm Raising a Teenager!_ is more than a plea for divine guidance through the maze of parenting. It is an honest account of a parent who has traveled through this painful yet rewarding path and, in spite of the obstacles, has successfully found the way to the other side. I am grateful to Bishop E. L. Warren for sharing the lessons that he, . . . Ella, and their wonderful children have learned. Throughout the book, Bishop Warren has presented what he calls "Sanity Sayings," which are principles that can be applied to the lives of all parents and to those who are not parents as well. Through this fantastic book, the Lord has sent help to those of us who are raising teenagers, and for that I say thank you!

Alfonzo K. Surrett, Jr.
Pastor and Founder
Kingdom Community Worship Center
Dolton, Illinois
Dean, South Suburban Christian Academy

Harvey, Illinois
President, Shofar Publications International
South Holland, Illinois

Raising children in today's society is a tremendous challenge. The various pressures of life coupled with an ungodly media that is constantly bombarding us can make it very difficult to produce godly seed. Thank God for Bishop Warren. He has written a powerful book. It is a very helpful tool to give us valuable insight in raising our children to fulfill their God-given destiny.

Richard Burruss
B.A., M.M., Ph.D. Student
Bishop, Transformation Christian Church and World Outreach Center
St. Louis, Missouri

If I had to take one book to partner with the Bible in serving as a foundation for the effective raising of a teenager, this would be the one.

Kevin Williams,
Teen Pastor, Cathedral of Worship
Quincy, Illinois

# CONTENTS

Dedication
Acknowledgments
Endorsements
Foreword
Introduction

# *FOREWORD*

I'm always leery of people who write about children and have never had any themselves. E. L. Warren is not only a great preacher, teacher, and pastor, but he and his wife are the parents of three teenagers. All of the three have now reached the age of maturity, but the journey was not easy.

In *Help, Lord! I'm Raising a Teenager!* I am especially impressed with his honesty in this important pursuit of parenthood. He says it like it is and brings wonderful observations. I particularly like the form in which the book is written. It is very clearly outlined and very easy reading. I love the "Sanity Sayings" and was complimented that he used one of mine. You will want to read very carefully Chapter Nine, where he lists the seven rules of teen life.

I certainly confirm his conclusion that a great revival is coming through the youth of our land. All of us as pastors, teachers, and parents should give support to this new generation with new vitality and creative ideas. This is a book you will want to read.

Archbishop Earl Paulk, Th.D., D.D.
The Cathedral at Chapel Hill
Decatur (Atlanta), Georgia

# INTRODUCTION

## *Babies Do Grow*

Unless there's a medical deficiency in your children, they will not stay infants but will one day develop into teenagers. The body will go through a metamorphosis, and the once flat-chested, straight-legged girl will become a full-breasted young woman with hips and lips. And that boy with zits will grow facial hair and muscles and will realize that mere thoughts can cause a physical change in his private parts.

So what do you do? Put them on pills? Buy a year's supply of condoms? Lock them in their room? Shut off the television and shield them from the opposite sex by using threats, fear, and superstition? Even if you do all of the above, sometimes the innocent fall prey, the naïve are taken advantage of, and the desirous, inquisitive children find a way to explore in their spare time.

We must first make sure to teach them the biblical values that support abstinence, virginity, and holiness. Second, we must make sure our home has a vast supply of love (more on this later), understanding, and conversation about the matters that ultimately involve every human being. Third, we must not be judgmental, comparative, suspicious, and paranoid. God will reveal, expose, and make known all truth and sin in time. Fourth, we must stay focused and help our teenagers stay focused. A mistake does not have to cost them their destiny. Lost virginity doesn't mean God changes His mind about them or their destiny.

Just as babies grow, teenagers grow. How we handle them will produce a behavior that will be passed down to *our* grandchildren. Let's make sure our teens see Jesus in us no matter what the situation produces. He knows all, forgives all, understands all, and loves us all.

## *SANITY SAYINGS !*

*Purpose is greater than sin,
and vision is greater than death.*

# 1

## TRAIN UP A CHILD IN THE WAY

*Train up a child in the way he should go:*
*and when he is old, he will not depart from it.*
Proverbs 22:6

*I am the way, the truth, and the life.*
John 14:6

O ur first assignment is to train our children in the *way,* in the lifestyle of Jesus. Training is a matter of discipline. Many of us adults have had little, if any, discipline and as a result find it hard to reproduce what's not present in our own lives. We were scolded, beaten, pushed, and told what we were and were not, but we were rarely trained in the ways of Jesus. Many adults today were never disciplined and find this concept uncomfortable. Most have learned by trial and error and, as a result, backslid at least once since confessing Jesus as Lord. Let me define backsliding. It's when you can remember a time that you were closer to God than you are now, and you're not doing anything to get back to that place.

Backsliding is not a single act. It's a series of wrong decisions or decisions contrary to the Word of

God. Generally, when we begin to backslide, we start by setting the Word of God to the side, or we cease to come into His presence first privately and then publicly.

We don't have to go backward! God is a forward-minded God. We can have as much of God as we want. He is "endless" (Heb. 7:16). And more than anything else, He offers us Himself to disciple us and to give clear guidelines designed to ensure continuous growth and victory in our lives and in our children's lives.

Many adults today went to church on Sundays and heard little, if any, truth and did what they wanted the rest of the week, only to return the next Sunday to repeat the cycle of deception. But our children need more. They need clear instruction. We should set a time to pray, a time to study, and a time to worship for them early in their lives so that when they get out on their own, it's a matter of habit! And we as adults should already have a set time for each of these areas in our lives. We instruct the pupil accordingly and require a regular progress report.

Our second assignment is to train them consistent with their *purpose* and *destiny*. This is where discernment, sensitivity, and wisdom come in on our part. We must get before God to know the way our children should go. Of course, they should go the way of Jesus Christ, but what about their God-given purpose and the God-ordained destinies for their lives?

All of our children may not naturally duplicate our choices of career and vocational preferences. That's okay because the right of the firstborn is the double portion (Deut. 21:17)! They will not only have traces of your spirit, gifts, and anointing, but they will possess their own unique gifts, calling, and anointing added to what they inherit from you. This is the double portion. They should exceed our effectiveness and level of success, and we should revel in their success. No father should be jealous of his children's success and accomplishments, but he should be proud and grateful for the hand of God.

After we have identified the way of purpose and the destiny of God for their lives, it's time to pray, get informed, and get prepared to assist them in reaching their expected end in a timely and orchestrated manner.

Purpose is why anyone or anything was created. It's what was in the mind of the Creator of the thing when the Creator of the thing created the thing.

Purpose can't be destroyed, but souls who fail to identify their purpose may be in for a long road of abuse because where purpose is not known, abuse is inevitable. To force a child into a career, sport, or academic preference based on the lives of the parents or the unfulfilled dreams of the parents is surely a set up for abuse. To pursue a career based purely on economic promise can be equally devastating. The hardest job anyone will ever do is the one he or she is not purposed to do.

## Set to Succeed or Fixed to Fail

*Having then gifts differing according*
*to the grace that is given to us.*
Romans 12:6

In addition to training our children in the way that they should go, we should set them in the graces where they will succeed. God has gifted every one of us by His grace or according to His favor to guarantee good success.

*This book of the law shall not depart out of thy mouth;*
*but thou shall meditate therein day and night,*
*that thou mayest observe to do according*
*to all that is written therein:*
*for then thou shalt make thy way prosperous,*
*and then thou shalt have good success.*
Joshua 1:8

Success is God's idea and His desire for *all* of His children. God Himself does not possess the capacity to fail and, therefore, by nature has graced all of His children to succeed.

One of the greatest challenges to the successful future of our teenagers is the unfulfilled past of the parent. Too many parents have watched their own lives slip away only to try to prolong them through the lives of their children. We want them to go to the school of our dreams, fulfill the unfulfilled dreams that we had, or even flow in the ministry that we never had.

Putting your children in vocations, careers, colleges, fields, or ministries that God has not graced for their gift is a set up for failure. When our egos and our desperation to see our unfulfilled dreams finished become more important than our teenagers' future, we fix them to fail. And if they develop a history of failure, they will become afraid of success or convinced that they're a failure and that success is for the rest of humanity. Why not discern, identify, and direct them into careers, ministries, and vocations that they are gifted for from birth? God gives gifts to every man according to *His* grace.

The motivational gifts of prophecy, ministry, teaching, exhorting, giving, ruling, and showing mercy are given by grace at birth (Romans 12:6-8). In

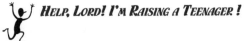 

this area of our gifting, we will naturally excel and succeed. God graced all people with *gifts* designed to make them who He intended them to be. With these gifts, we are all set up to succeed.

Everyone is born an original; I've been gifted by grace to be the best *me* anyone could *be*. So take some time to identify the areas of *giftedness* in your teenagers and then discuss with them, their school counselor, and your pastor the best route for their lives to ensure success rather than failure.

# SANITY SAYINGS !

*I am the best me anyone could ever be.*

Now, together with your spouse and children, pray and seek God for His purpose in your children's lives. Then train your children in the *way*, identify their purpose and areas of grace *giftedness*, and watch them experience their destiny.

Destiny is wherever God commands us to be. Too many children end up provoked due to unrealistic expectations and lives that pursue purposes and destinies that are not their own. We want our children to succeed even if it's in a purpose and career other than what we in our natural minds would have chosen for them.

# Sanity Sayings !

*You will lose some battles because some things are only learned in lost battles.*

*Character is built in crisis.*

*Sin can always breed where self lives.*

# 2

## MY CHILD IS NOT A VIRGIN ANYMORE

In the act of intercourse, two become one, and souls are joined, bringing with them all of their baggage—good, bad, or indifferent.

> And when Shechem the son of Hamor the Hivite, prince of the country, saw her, he took her, and lay with her, and defiled her. And his soul clave unto Dinah the daughter of Jacob, and he loved the damsel. And Shechem spake unto his father Hamor, saying, Get me this damsel to wife. And Jacob heard that he had defiled Dinah his daughter: now his sons were with his cattle in the field: and Jacob held his peace until they were come. And Hamor the father of Shechem went out unto Jacob to commune with him. And the sons of Jacob came out of the field when they heard *it:* and the men were grieved, and they were very wroth, because he had wrought folly in Israel in lying with Jacob's daughter; which thing ought not

to be done. And Hamor communed with them, saying, The soul of my son Shechem longeth for your daughter: I pray you give her him to wife. And make ye marriages with us: *and* give your daughters unto us, and take our daughters unto you. And ye shall dwell with us: and the land shall be before you; dwell and trade ye therein, and get you possessions therein. And Shechem said unto her father and unto her brethren, Let me find grace in your eyes, and what ye shall say unto me I will give. Ask me never so much dowry and gift, and I will give according as ye shall say unto me: but give me the damsel to wife. (Gen. 34:2-12)

After Shechem took Dinah his soul *clave* unto her. The word *clave* in the Hebrew language is *dabaq*, which means to be joined together. This joining together of souls is why premarital, extramarital, casual, and addictive sexual relationships enslave many in a trap that some never get out of. It's a viscous cycle of emotional peaks and valleys. God intended for the act of intercourse to join two for life, not for a night! If your teenager is in an unlawful relationship, victory is on its way. Read on! (Unlawful means it is not the will of God, nor is it leading to the will of God.)

First, we must eliminate desire and opportunity to satisfy the desire. The desire will die if it has no way to access what it wants. (Note: If it is a spirit, it must be cast out as well! In order to get victory, we must eliminate both.) Since accessibility is a variable that is sometimes beyond our control, desire is where we should effectively target the anointing for deliverance. Jesus said, "If thy hand offend thee, cut it off: it is better for thee to enter into life maimed, than having two hands to go into hell, into the fire that never shall be quenched (Mark 9:43).

Eliminate anything that contributes to desires that draw you from God. Desire left undetected creates cravings, which if left uncorrected create habits that produce addiction, which produces bondage that is passed on from generation to generation. To correct this web of bondage it generally takes time to reprogram the mind.

A desire can be denied for thirty days, and it will not become a craving. A craving must be resisted ninety days, and it will not become a habit. A habit must be broken by failure to repeat it for six months, and it will not become an addiction. An addiction needs to be starved for one year, and we will have loosed ourselves from bondage. Certainly, there are exceptions to these timetables. There are times when the anointing comes upon you, and freedom is received instantly without any tendency for relapse. Once free at any level, you must *resist the devil* to successfully retain your victory.

In order to starve the desires of your flesh, you must deny your *self,* not self-denial but deny *self!* Tell self no, emphatically NO! Deny self anything that gives it additional strength to resist God's will. Many times people fast—starve the body (belly)—but feed the flesh (carnality, television, and other pleasures that leave self in its place of authority). We must attack ungodly desires if we are ever going to walk in continuous victory over unlawful relationships.

**God Has a Plan.**

Sex is God's idea. It is the God-created vehicle ordained to consummate the union of a man and a woman who have committed themselves in marriage. Let's talk about the steps of a lawful or quality relationship that is the will of God.

So many men feel that sex is everything, and most women vehemently disagree. What about romance and affection? What about conversation? What about friendship? What about love? Real love can't wait to give and always seeks an avenue of expression, but lust can't wait to get. We need a clear definition of *infatuation* and *love*. According to *Webster's Dictionary and Thesaurus,* infatuation is defined as fascination, captivation, passion, crush, fanaticism, obsession, and idolatry. Love desires to give when your attraction has matured first to friendship, then to emotion, next to commitment, and finally to intimacy. Your desire is not to satisfy yourself but to extend yourself to the one you love enough to give yourself to. Love gives (can't wait to give); lust takes (can't wait to get). Love sees flaws and still loves.

## Five Steps to a Lawful Quality Relationship and Marriage

1. Attraction: Spiritually or physically
   *Agapao:* Social moral love
2. Friendship: Sharing
   *Koinonea:* Sharing
3. Emotions: Caring
   *Phileo:* Fond love
4. Commitment: Marriage
   *Agape:* Sacrificial love
5. Intimacy: Consummation of the first four
   *Eros:* Physical love

Most people go from step one to step five, skipping the steps in between, and set themselves up to live a miserable, crippled life for years. When everything is according to God's plan, sex is a wonderful expression of the love the man has for his wife and the submission the wife has for her husband.

*Drink waters out of thine own cistern,*
*and running waters out of thine own well.*
*Let thy fountains be dispersed abroad,*
*and rivers of waters in the streets.*
*Let them be only thine own,*
*and not strangers' with thee.*
*Let thy fountain be blessed:*
*and rejoice with the wife of thy youth.*
Proverbs 5:15-20

You are somebody's refreshment. A cistern is a covered well or a tank that stores water. A well is an open source of water. "Drink waters out of thine own cistern, and running waters out of thine own well" (Prov. 5:15). If you're not married, you have not become the owner of (I Cor. 7) or the covering for the well (I Cor. 11:3-8). A cistern must be replenished, and only the husband, the cistern's covering, can replenish that which was removed.

## Don't Be Deceived.

"But we love each other." We hear this line after the admission of premature, premarital, casual, or addictive sex. We also hear, "Can we just be friends?" and "We're getting married." Here's the litmus test: What God joins, let no man put asunder; what God doesn't join, let no man put together.

A marriage made out of the mistakes of a moment many times is short lived and full of instability because the foundation is substandard. One mistake is enough. Don't let your teenagers make another by marrying someone who is not God's perfect will. God's plan and the destiny of God for their lives have not changed. Now you must resist the desire to construct something based on the present situation and on the fear that what God had planned has changed.

If his children forsake My law, and walk not in My judgments; If they break My statutes, and keep not My commandments; Then will I visit their transgression with the rod, and their iniquity with stripes. Nevertheless My lovingkindness will I not utterly take from him, nor suffer My faithfulness to fail. My covenant will I not break, nor alter the thing that is gone out of My lips. Once have I sworn by My holiness that I will not lie unto David.(Psalms 89:30-35)

## *SANITY SAYINGS !*

*Fear is the mother of panic and the precursor of bad decisions.*

## God Chastens But Never Changes!

The judgment of God *does not* cancel the promises of God! God makes *no* promise to us based on the arm of our flesh! All of God's judgments and corrections proceed out of His love for us but never negate His promises to us.

## Crossing the Line of Intimacy

Now, about the idea of just being friends, once friends cross the line of intimacy, they can never go back to just being friends. You'll *never* just be friends again. The line of intimacy should only be crossed in marriage, and if we cross it outside of marriage or before marriage with anyone, it puts the relationship on another level, never to be just friends again! And in the case of incest, the parent-child relationship is damaged, and sometimes the child is destroyed. Certainly, their childhood is lost forever. So, to the teenager, I say repent! To those in unlawful sexual relationships, repent and pray this prayer.

*Lord Jesus,*

*Have mercy upon me. I have sinned against heaven and brought reproach and grief to the kingdom of God, my family, and myself. I refuse to let the enemy win the war. Forgive me, wash me, loose me from this relationship and the desire for anything other than Your will. And help me as I resist the devil to walk in victory from this day forward. In Jesus' name, I pray. Amen.*

## A Final Note on Repentance

*Bring forth therefore fruits meet for repentance.*
Matthew. 3:8

True repentance bears fruit. When God has worked a work in us and worked on us, the normal process of succession is repentance from dead works and then the fruit of that repentance—turning back to God. When a heart is truly repentant, no one has to say do this or do that. You, from the joy of knowing you're forgiven and no longer judged and condemned to bear the penalty for your sin, automatically respond with action that reflects a repentant heart.

And Jesus entered and passed through Jericho. And, behold, there was a man named Zaccheus, which was the chief among the publicans, and he was rich. And he sought to see Jesus who He was: and could not for the press, because he was little of stature. And He ran before, and climbed up into a sycomore tree to see Him: for He was to pass that way. And when Jesus came to the place, He looked up, and saw him, and said unto him, Zaccheus, make haste, and come down; for today I must abide at thy house. And he made haste, and came down, and received Him joyfully. And when they saw it, they all murmured, saying, That He was gone to be guest with a man that is a sinner. And Zaccheus stood, and said unto the Lord; Behold, Lord, the half of my goods I give to the poor; and if I have taken any thing from any man by false accusation, I restore him fourfold. And Jesus said unto him, This day is salvation come to this house, forsomuch as he also is a son of Abraham. (Luke 19:1-9)

True repentance positions us to become fruitful again.

> He spake also this parable; A cer-
> tain man had a fig tree planted in his
> vineyard; and he came and sought fruit
> thereon, and found none. Then said he
> unto the dresser of his vineyard, Behold,
> these three years I come seeking fruit on
> this fig tree, and find none: cut it down;
> why cumbereth it the ground? And he
> answering said unto him, Lord, let it
> alone this year also, till I shall dig about
> it, and dung it: And if it bear fruit, well:
> and if not, then after that thou shalt cut
> it down. (Luke 13:6-9)

Sometimes our lives are not as fruitful as God intended, and we are not or are no longer walking in the potential that God has placed in our lives. So God *dungs* our lives, orders mess into our lives, and through the mess, trial, and testing comes forth a brokenness, a revealing of our real nature and extreme need for God. We cry out with a repentant heart and bear fruit unto righteousness.

## Suggestions

- Talk to your children about sex and the responsibility of parenting.
- Tell your children when they're young, "I love you."
- Enter a covenant with them, a covenant of abstinence, offer them a covenant token—a ring for girls and a chain for boys—and add a diamond or enlarge the stone each year to celebrate their life of abstinence and virginity.
- Keep the lines of communication open. Honest communication will always provide a venue for discussing the delicate matters of teenage life.

## *SANITY SAYINGS !*

*Our actions are the true indications of our beliefs.*

*Purpose never changes.*

# *3*

## *DISCIPLINING CHILDREN*

Children should be loved, nurtured, trained, and raised in a safe, Bible-based Christian environment. Each child must be given a clear set of rules and the impending consequences for breaking them. Remember that consistency from year to year (or decade to decade) is important, especially in homes with more than one child. Many times rules that are made for the oldest are in consideration of how the youngest will handle the same challenges when he or she finally arrives at the age of the oldest.

When rules are broken, the prescribed punishment must be imposed. God is clear in stating the need for the rod (Proverbs 13:24, 19:18, 22:15, 23:13, and 29:15). Therefore, a rod (a belt or paddle) should be used but never the hand. Our hands are to constantly represent love, caring, and covering. So whenever punishment is required, always follow the chastening with a hug of affirmation so that chastening is associated with love. Never discipline a child when you are too angry or too tired to reason.

Children are a blessing and can either give you much joy or much grief, and it all depends on you the parent. They will do what you do, not only what you say. A strong, consistent Christian witness will produce the same in children that are raised in such a healthy environment. Discipline and parental nurture are the two most important formative factors in all of life. Healthy attitudes are caught, not just taught.

I question some of the new techniques of discipline: time outs, no contact chastening, and punishments that take away privileges. If we love our children and if the Bible is the law of our home, then the techniques that God spells out are sure to prove more effective than something we have developed through our human reasoning.

## Developing a Good Work Ethic

*For even when we were with you,*
*this we commanded you,*
*that if any would not work, neither should he eat.*
II Thessalonians 3:10

If a man will not work, he shall not eat. The purpose of work is not to make money but to complete a job. Compensation is the reward given for the skill, detail, and time absorbed while doing the job.

Many teenagers arrive at their job interview at two o'clock dressed in the latest sleeveless attire complimented by sagging jeans, dark shades, and no resume. When we give money for no service rendered, no skill employed, or no time absorbed, we negate the purpose for work, developing a poor work ethic in our teenager. We need to help develop our teenagers in this area.

I suggest that children should work in the home and should be compensated; they should be given an allowance. But never give money without money being the payment for service rendered, excluding birthdays and special occasions. Of course, I'm speaking of children who are old enough to do chores responsibly and selective enough to want certain fashions and toys.

According to *The Millionaire Mind* by Thomas Stanley, Ph.D., most millionaires who scored under a hundred on their Scholastic Achievement Test discovered that hard work was more important than high intelligence in achieving success. And sixty-one percent of these same millionaires said being well disciplined was a factor in attaining economic success.

If we consistently levy proper discipline and live a constant Christian life in front of our children, most of the rebellion will be driven out of them before they're teenagers. But be prepared for times of testing. Teenagers have the outside influence of peers, the inward influence of hormones, and the mental confusion of thinking they're grown and should be treated as an adult yet have all the amenities of a child. Again, when rules are broken, the prescribed punishment must be imposed.

*Foolishness is bound in the heart of a child;*
*but the rod of correction shall drive it far from him.*
Proverbs 22:15

Now they are six-feet, two-inches tall, can bench-press you, and eat a week's worth of groceries in two days. So firmness, consistency, and follow-through are a must. A belt may not be painful, but removing the phone from their room, denying them the privilege of going to the homecoming football game, or denying some other privilege is a *blow* to their ego that may prove more painful than a rod.

However, we don't want to break their spirit.

*The spirit of a man will sustain his infirmity;*
*but a wounded spirit who can bear?*
Proverbs 18:14

But we must consistently break their will. That's the only way they will ever yield totally to the will of God in their lives.

## Leave the Rest to God.

Some may say, "But I was not a believer during the most impressionable years of my children's lives, so they are only acting out of the environment they were raised in." To you I say, "Trust in the LORD with all thine heart; and lean not unto thine own understanding" (Proverbs 3:5). God is able to show Himself in a way that will make a strong enough impression that a decision to change or at least an acknowledgment that God is real is inevitable.

As parents, we must avoid hypocrisy in any degree. We must live what we preach and be what we profess at home, in our community, and in our conversation. In homes where there's partiality and hypocrisy, children will not possess much respect for you or for what you preach as the Christian standard.

Finally, disciplining biblically keeps the matter of correction a family matter. Punishment lets what should be a family matter become a community matter because everyone knows the rules were broken and consequences were applied. As mentioned earlier, now that they're football defensive lineman or runner-up for prom queen, other appropriate measures will prove most effective.

The Bible is clear about why discipline is necessary. To not discipline is to not *love,* and this com-

bination will produce rebellious, disrespectful, and ungrateful children. Eventually, living without discipline will prove more destructive than the temporary pain that would have been experienced through the disciplinary action.

## Setting a Standard

There must be a clear standard set for our children. God is a God of standards. When the enemy comes in like a flood, the Lord shall raise up a standard (Isaiah 59:19). Without a standard, what does God have to raise against our enemy? In every one of our lives there must be enough Word that in a crisis or an unexpected scenario—a hit from the blind side—God can raise up by the Word in us and the convictions of that Word a standard against the enemy of our souls.

God is a God of standards. He is never ever nervous about sin. God never judges us for what we've done but rather for what we refuse to become. God did not destroy Sodom and Gomorrah due to sin but because there was no clear standard of the kingdom of God. Where are the King's kids? Where are the righteous?

- One can put one thousand to flight (Deuteronomy 32:30)!
- If any two touch and agree, it shall be (Matthew 18:19)!
- "The effectual, fervent prayer of a righteous man availeth much" (James 5:16)!

When there is no conviction, no standard, God responds in judgment. But again I remind you, God never judges us for what we've done but for what we refuse to become. His judgment and correction proceed out of His love for us. And without a clear standard, we may win a battle, but we're sure to lose the war.

# Sanity Sayings !

*Vision sees what others can't see
even when you're looking at the same thing.*

*Every trial has an expiration date.*
—Job

*The focused find a way to find their way.*

*Diversity embraced is unity achieved.*
—Harold Ray

*Never fight a battle you don't have to win.*

# 4

## *TRANSITION TO DESTINY*

One day your teenagers walk in and have an earring in their tongue, a tattoo on their thigh or neck, green dye in their hair, and the smell of marijuana on their clothes! Your first reaction—after the initial shock—is to throw them to the floor, scrub them clean, yank out the earrings, and beat the snot out of them while telling them they're destroying themselves and you're not going to allow it. So they run away from home. Now what?

The Hebrew writer reminds us of what Jesus did to survive the destruction en route to His destiny, "who for the joy that was set before Him endured the cross" (Hebrews 12:2). We must remember what we saw in the spirit about our children, what was prophesied over them, what we believe to be their purpose and their destiny, and look at that, not them, during this time of transition. Remember why you came into the earth and why they came into the earth. Remember where you're going in God and where they're going in God. Their destiny hasn't changed, and their purpose never changes. His promises haven't changed. Their call hasn't changed. Your call hasn't changed, and God hasn't changed. So in spite

of what you're looking at, stay focused! The goal is still there! Satan is counting on you getting distracted, growing discouraged, and giving up; many parents do. Consequently, neither they nor their children ever reach their "expected end" (Proverbs 23:18). The focused find a way to find their way. The focused find a way to the goal.

Jesus never wavered. As He went toward Calvary, there were many distractions—attempts to get Him to detour—but the goal was clear to Him because it was clear in Him.

Our children have a destiny. The enemy laughs hysterically when one of them detours, defects, trips, or falls. Then if they have little or no support, they're lost for a lifetime as they drift into the ruin of Satan's intended plot. And when parents care more for their egos and their reputations than for their children, they can blow the opportunity to heal the hurting, to pick up the discarded, and to build in their children a bond of trust and character that they'll carry for a lifetime. Remember that character is built in crisis. Bonding emotionally is a part of building quality relationships.

An abandonment of purpose is an abandonment of God's power. Remember that purpose is greater than sin, and life outside purpose is the equivalent of death. We must help our children identify and fortify their purpose. Everyone is born with a purpose, and if we live and die without discovering that purpose, it still will never negate the fact that we came to earth with a purpose. You can't destroy purpose, but a life without purpose is easily destroyed. Purpose has no law, but no law can order success to a life without purpose.

As often as opportunity allows, remind them of their purpose. Remind yourself of their purpose. Keep the line of communication open, so there is a connection to someone connected to the life of God. We need a continuous flow of God's power into and through our life into their life to deal with every crisis and every success that will come to a life connected to God's purpose.

One of the more subtle attempts of Satan to shipwreck our teenagers is to lure them off the path of God's perfect will with false futures. The teenage years are some of the most delicate and impressionable times in one's life. Dreams, big-city opportunities, career promises, and the pressures of *Ishmael* relationships can set a decoy in their path, and without proper counsel, they can spend months or years chasing a false future.

## What's Really at Stake?

◆　　Your dreams or theirs?
◆　　Your future or theirs?
◆　　Your career or theirs?
◆　　Your ego or theirs?
◆　　Your name or theirs?
◆　　Your goals and aspirations or theirs?

Please pause and answer these questions honestly. Caution must be exercised here because many times we rush to draw the line, set limits, and exact limitations that, if we're not careful, will provoke our teenager to wrath.

*And, ye fathers, provoke not your children to wrath:*
*but bring them up in the nurture*
*and admonition of the Lord.*
Ephesians 6:4

*Can two walk together, except they be agreed?*
Amos 3:3

Our teenagers' hormones are peeking. Their popularity is rising. The demands associated with being a teen; being a Christian; being popular; being attractive; and wanting to obey you, please the cheerleader, and be the "A" student who gets the family select seats at the baccalaureate program has pimples and tempers at a bursting point. Take a deep breath and remind yourself of the prophecies that have been uttered and the destiny of which God has assured you for them and for you.

*This charge I commit unto thee, son Timothy,*
*according to the prophecies which went before on thee,*
*that thou by them mightest war a good warfare;*
*Holding faith, and a good conscience;*
*which some having put away,*
*concerning faith have made shipwreck.*
I Timothy 1:18-19

Now set your face like flint toward God and then stand and take aim at the real enemy, Satan. Sometimes lines, limits, and legislation only widen the gap between our teenager and us at a time when they need us the most. So don't take yourself or them so seriously. Remember that you were a teenager once and have blossomed into a successful adult, and so will they. I know, you want to keep them from making the mistakes that you made and from being hurt like you were, and I applaud your parental prowess. There will be times when we can connect with our teenagers and guide them around the pitfalls of pre-adulthood. But even if we don't, God will *keep* everything and everyone that we commit to Him!

*Commit thy way unto the LORD;
trust also in him; and he shall bring it to pass.*
Psalm 37:5

**God Will Steer the Rudder of Their Heart.**

You train them up in the *way* and live a clear
Christian standard before them. When they seem to
be shipwrecking, all that you have taught them will
keep them and will comfort you. God is still steering
the rudder of their heart and will bring them to their
expected end.

*There are many devices in a man's heart;
nevertheless the counsel of the LORD, that shall stand.*
Proverbs 19:21

Only the purpose of God shall stand. So buy
the truth, and sell it not (Proverbs 23:23). Then guide
your heart in the way of your destiny because your
destiny and their destiny is real (Proverbs 23:19), and
trust God to get your teenager to theirs. Destiny is
being wherever God commands. Vision is the ability
to see your destiny. Surely there is an end, a true
future, for our teenagers' life (Proverbs 23:18). Our
job is to help them identify paths of truth that lead to
their expected end. This is where the wisdom of God

must be sought, discernment received, and patience employed.

*For I know the thoughts that I think toward you,
saith the LORD, thoughts of peace,
and not of evil, to give you an expected end.*
Jeremiah 29:11

Remind yourself and your teenagers that their destiny is sure! Their end is expecting them, their future is true, and God is God!

**Destiny is a Matter of Choice.**
        We are shaping a generation. When you feel like saying, "What's the use? Why bother? He's just like his dad. She's just like her mom," remember that destiny is a matter of choice.
        We're shaping a generation that is set on breaking all the rules and leaving their tracks in the sands of history. Set a standard because people always rise to a true expectation. Let your teenager know why character is important and why you've set a clear standard. Then pray and believe in faith that he or she will attain the goals set.

## <u>*Sanity Sayings !*</u>

*Victory comes to the prepared.*
—Earl Paulk

*Life is filled with opportunities daily.*
*But only the prepared can turn*
*opportunities into victories.*

**Final Note: "Everybody else will be there. Everybody is doing it."**

Repeatedly our teens try to play the guilt card on us and make us believe that our convictions are about thirty years off pace. They say, "Times have changed. I'm the only one in my class who . . ."

Take courage. You have the distinct responsibility before God to raise *your* children and lead *your* teenager. And when they're old, they and you will be glad that a clear standard was set and that character was birthed in their lives because they'll reproduce in your grandchildren what they learned.

# 5

# THERE'S A REVIVAL COMING!

*Ye shall not see wind, neither shall ye see rain;*
*yet that valley shall be filled with water.*
II Kings 3:17

*And he shall turn the heart of the fathers*
*to the children,*
*and the heart of the children to their fathers.*
Malachi 4:6

A revival is generally universal in application, reproducible by faith, and validated by biblical precepts and principles; it transcends the time frame of the initial occurrence. This revival that I envision will encompass the world. In my travel I meet teenagers, young adults from all nations, that seem to have similar challenges, aspirations, and conflicts. Perhaps this is the reason God has chosen to bring revival through our home. God uses crisis to persuade communication and produce character, and character and communication are bringing families to a place of revival. Revival is a coming back to Jesus Christ.

Most are looking to Christian TV, to another conference, or to some Christian personality for the embers of revival, but I believe there's a revival being birthed in homes across the world. Families are finding themselves in places where without God they would crack and begin to blame or condemn. The crisis is forcing them to communicate, and the communication is producing character. The character is revealing the need to get back to Jesus Christ.

## The Power of Communication

What is communication? Communication is the art of transmitting and receiving information in a way that causes understanding to be gained from what was said or done. If we're to succeed in raising our children in life and in society, improvement in this area is a must. We take our example from God.

God speaks on all frequencies to insure that all can understand what He wills and wants for and from their lives. God the Father and Jesus exemplify the quality of communication that we all must strive for:

◆ He only did what He saw the Father do.
◆ He only said what He heard the Father say.
◆ God always spoke on the frequency of the hearer: to Pharaoh He spoke, showed, touched; to Moses He showed, spoke, and touched.

## Communication Frequencies

God deals with all people based on the frequencies He gave them. Frequency is the God-given ability in individuals to transmit and receive information in a way unique to them. Audio people hear God. Visual people see God. Kinesthetic (feeling) people sense God. For example, Peter's frequency was audio.

*And he **said** unto Him, Lord,*
*I am ready to go with Thee,*
*both into prison, and to death.*
Luke 22:33

*But go your way, **tell** His disciples and*
*Peter that He goeth before you into Galilee: there*
*shall ye see Him, as He **said** unto you.*
Mark 16:7

Adam, also, was audio.

*And the LORD God commanded the man, **saying,***
*Of every tree of the garden thou mayest freely eat.*
Genesis 2:16

Joshua, on the other hand, was visual.

> *On that day the LORD magnified Joshua in the*
> ***sight*** *of all Israel;*
> *and they feared him, as they feared Moses,*
> *all the days of his life.*
> Joshua 4:14

> *And the LORD said unto Joshua,* ***See,*** *I have given*
> *into thine hand Jericho,*
> *and the king thereof, and the mighty men of valour.*
> Joshua 6:2

And Jesus' mother, Mary, was kinesthetic.

> *And the angel came in unto her, and said,*
> *Hail,* ***thou that art*** *highly* ***favored,***
> *the Lord* ***is*** *with thee: blessed* ***art*** *thou among women.*
> *And when she saw him, she was* ***troubled*** *at his saying,*
> *and cast* ***in her mind*** *what manner of*
> *salutation this should be.*
> *And the angel said unto her,* ***Fear*** *not, Mary:*
> *for thou hast found* ***favor*** *with God.*
> Luke 1:28-30

> *And Mary said, My* ***soul*** *doth* ***magnify*** *the Lord.*
> Luke 1:46

Everyone has both an internal and an external frequency. We receive on our internal frequency and transmit on our external frequency. Peter, Adam, Noah, Joshua, and Mary all transmitted and received on their primary frequency. However, some individuals transmit on one frequency and receive on another. The apostle Paul was internally visual and externally audio.

*And as he journeyed, he came near Damascus:*
*and suddenly there shined round about him*
*a **light** from heaven: And he fell to the earth,*
*and **heard a voice saying** unto him, Saul, Saul,*
*why persecutest Thou Me?  And he said,*
*Who art Thou, Lord?  And the Lord said, I am*
*Jesus whom thou persecutest:*
***it is** hard for thee to kick against the pricks.*
*And he trembling and astonished **said**,*
*Lord, what wilt Thou have me to do?*
Acts 9:3-6

Likewise, David was internally visual but externally kinesthetic.

*And it came to pass, after the year was expired,*
*at the time when kings go forth **to battle**,*

*that David sent Joab, and his servants with him,
and all Israel; and they destroyed the children of
Ammon, and besieged Rabbah.  But David tarried
still at Jerusalem. And it came to pass in an
eveningtide, that David arose from off his bed,
and walked upon the roof of the king's house:
and from the roof he **saw** a woman washing herself;
and the woman **was very beautiful to look upon.***
II Samuel 11:1-2

## Unique Combinations of Communication Frequencies

### 1. Internal Feeling and External Audio

These people will measure and weigh your
words by their feelings. If they're hurt, they'll tear
you to pieces verbally and let feelings keep them
from saying they're wrong. If they're talking to an
internal feeling person, they could shred that person's
feelings and say, "Boy, you sure are sensitive." If
they're hurt or disappointed, they'll weep, but their
response is to the point and matter of fact. Also,
when you ask them what is going on, they feel like
they must tell you in full detail. If these people stop
communicating, they'll be non-verbal, will start
reacting with some form of body language such as the
loss of a smile, and could be a bomb waiting to go
off.

## 2.   Internal Visual and External Feeling

Progress is ascertained in physical signs, and this combination will cry if it appears they can't make progress. Their feelings will show easily and readily. If they stop communicating, they will become introverted and cold. King David portrays this combination.

## 3.   Internal Audio and External Visual

These individuals will measure you by what you say. They measure their own words carefully. They are people of few words but will speak if given time. When they speak, they usually use hands and visual gestures. If these people stop communicating, they may let their appearance and surroundings get away from them.

## Danger Zones

Audio people are prone to gossip and hearsay, missing visual signs and over-reacting to statements. Visual people see what they shouldn't and misread verbal signs. They are prone to pursue vision without preparation. They may miss verbal warnings or go overboard with their actions. With kinesthetic people, feelings may get out of control. They might miss visual signs and verbal warnings. They can be driven by feelings.

HELP, LORD! I'M RAISING A TEENAGER!

## Communion

Webster's Dictionary defines communion as sharing, possessing one's thoughts and emotions in common, and participating.

*But if we walk in the light, as He is in the light, we have fellowship one with another, and the blood of Jesus Christ His Son cleanseth us from all sin.*
I John 1:7

Here, the Greek word for fellowship, *koinonia*, means partnership, participation, and communion. Communion invites communication. Communication without communion gives birth to discussions that are instructional and condescending.

## Actions Speak

All actions speak but at times don't communicate. In other words, I know what you said, but did you mean what your actions really said about what you are saying?

## Silence

Silence speaks but doesn't communicate.

58

## God, The Master Communicator

God is a master communicator, using words, illustrations, and expressions to leave no room for misunderstanding how He feels about us and what His plan and purpose is for us. The Bible opens with "God said." Whatever God wants is inside what He's speaking to and comes out of what He spoke to, to become what He said (Mark 11:24). We have what we say. Most want something other than what they're speaking but are only getting what they're saying.

Every human being has a God-given frequency, even our children! Take some time to identify the communication frequency of everyone in your family. How? Listen to their choice of words. For example, visual communicators use these phrases: "I see" and "It's clear." Audio communicators use these: "Listen to me" and "You didn't hear me" and "I'm talking." Kinesthetic communicators use these phrases: "You don't care" and "You really don't understand." Watch body language and eyes as well. Visual communicators will use hand gestures while kinesthetic people will touch. Audio people might strike or pound the table when speaking. (This chapter is by no means an exhaustive teaching on communication, so I strongly recommend my audio six-tape teaching series called Communication.)

## Revival Is on the Way.

Now that we're communicating, make sure the Word of God has a place in the discussion. Get ready, the valley is about to fill with living water, and revival is breaking forth in your home!

Some parents try to talk using the words of their teenagers, but even if you talk like them, you may not be communicating with them. These teenage years, believe it or not, are as complicated for them as they are for you. So make some time and take some time to spend with them because if they're not talking to you, they're talking to someone else or talking to themselves.

Faith comes by hearing (Romans 10:17), even when we're hearing the wrong thing. We parents should be clear in communicating our beliefs, convictions, goals, and expectations for our children. But also be realistic and flexible when they communicate theirs. Don't be so quick to write them off as failures because at this point they see the world differently, and they want to contribute their efforts in a way that doesn't follow your plans for their life.

It's up to you to restrain your negative statements and instead offer supportive and constructive suggestions. Your comments weigh heavy on the mind of your teenager. So measure your words by the potential you see in them and the incredible future that God has for them. Your teenagers can succeed if you train them to master their strengths. Teens who are not analytically intelligent may be technical geniuses. Those who may not be pastors may be tremendous organizers for great pastors.

As you communicate, listen well to their heart and continuously solicit wisdom from God. What we say can be the difference in our teenager succeeding or failing.

**Final Note on Revival**

Our teenagers will never catch what hasn't caught us. Most of what they learn is more caught than taught. If you want them to be on fire, sold out, dedicated, studious, compassionate, and understanding, first *you* try to be all of these!

## *Sanity Sayings !*

*The fight is fixed. Though you may lose some battles, the war is already won.*

# 6

## Guard Your Hearts

Though no parent wants to believe that their sweet, cuddly, seven-pound baby could have somehow become the haven for demonic spirits, the truth is sometimes it happens. Though innocent, vulnerable, and naïve, they sometimes become the prey for an enemy that has no respect of persons. If your teenager becomes reclusive, defiant, unusually rebellious, full of hate, and full of rage and shows tendencies of destruction either to themselves or to others, we must consider the possibility of satanic infringement.

Now before we call the priest or the pastor to perform an exorcism, let's become a bit more informed. Have your teenagers been listening to hard rock or heavy metal music filled with lyrics that promote violence and rebellion? Have they become friends with peers who are anti-social, anti-establishment, anti-Christian, and *anti-anti?* Have they become interested in death, pain, morbidity, or the occult? What type of magazines, movies, and books are they reading? And don't forget to check the history on your browser to see what addresses they are frequenting on the Internet.

If your investigation proves positive involvement or casual inquisition, your first step is to pray and ask God for wisdom, discernment, and courage. You are the parent and have the spiritual authority to evict any and every trespassing spirits, and they must obey you in Jesus' name.

Your prayer time may reveal that your teenagers' interests are providing the avenue for Satan's influence. Measures such as burning the books and throwing away the videos and scrubbing off the tattoo will not correct the problem. We must identify the strongman! No, we don't converse with demons; they all lie. But God will reveal the spiritual strongman that we're confronting, and He and His anointing are stronger than he that is in the world or in your teenager. Once we know with whom we're dealing, we call him by name and demand him to go back to the pit of hell in Jesus' name, and he must obey us. Depending on his level of involvement with your teenager, mind renewal and behavior monitoring and modification may be necessary, but the root (the cause) for the behavior is evicted!

## It's Your House.

It's your house, they're your children, and *you* have the right to go into their room, check out their music, see what they're watching on TV, monitor their friends, and do whatever else the spirit of God prompts you to do. Your teenager has no idea of how subtle, destructive, and seductive Satan can be. Parental negligence could destroy teenagers and land them in a place that you, as a parent, would never have believed possible.

For an in-depth teaching on casting out demons, please order my audio six-tape series entitled "Unmasking Satan." Request the manual and the flash cards for an exhaustive teaching on the subject of casting out devils. Don't panic or become fearful or anxious.

*Be careful for nothing; but in every thing by prayer and*
*supplication with thanksgiving*
*let your requests be made known unto God.*
*And the peace of God,*
*which passeth all understanding, shall keep your hearts*
*and minds through Christ Jesus.*
Philippians 4:6-7 (KJV)

*Do not be anxious about anything, but in everything, by*
*prayer and petition, with thanksgiving, present your*
*requests to God. And the peace of God,*
*which transcends all understanding, will guard your*
*hearts and your minds in Christ Jesus.*
Philippians 4:6-7 (NIV)

Our war is with an enemy who is destructive, deliberate, patient, and shrewd. But he is keenly aware that he is no match for anyone under the anointing of God. Ecclesiates 8:11 explains that we must sentence every evil work speedily so that the heart is not fully set in them to do evil.

## The Deceitfulness of the Heart

The heart is wicked in and of itself. Demons live and breed where darkness and sin are, so make sure you have exposed every possible breeding ground or attempt of the enemy to rule in the life of your teenager.

# 7

## *Desert or Destiny?*

*Now it's off to college, university,
trade school, or military service.*

N ow What? After we have narrowed down our
choices of schools or military service, the area
should be canvassed to identify a church that can support the principles, standards, and Christian values
that have been a part of their lives for the past seventeen or more years.

It's a mistake to send your child off to an area
that is spiritually deficient. Slowly but certainly, the
lack of spiritual nutrition will lead to an erosion of the
standards previously set and give opportunity for the
enemy to set traps to which they will eventually fall
prey. If the area is spiritually deficient, choose another area. Please don't send them into a spiritual desert
only to become the food for the vultures of their soul.

*Righteousness exalteth a nation:
but sin is a reproach to any people.*
Proverbs 14:34

In places where the body of Christ is strong and effective, there will be signs in the natural: economic empowerment, reduced crime, harmony among pastors, church and government partnering for safe communities, growing churches, and an overall sense of the peace of God resting on the city. To leave your children in a place that is spiritually deserted is carelessness and reckless parenting. This kind of irresponsibility will produce negative consequences that will grieve our hearts in days to come.

## Recommendations

◆ No dating. Relationships that are exclusive with the opposite sex and that have not been identified as to their purpose and contribution to the will of God are time bombs waiting to go off. (Please re-read Chapter 2.) Excessive phone conversations, chunks of time that can not be accounted for, and evasive conversations are all warnings that something is already in the making.

◆ Cell phones, pagers, long-distance calling cards, and privileges should be carefully considered before being awarded to your teenagers. These luxuries or amenities only add to the plethora of distractions facing our teenagers in this new environment.

## A Whole New World

For most teenagers, this is their first time away from home, the city or town in which they grew up, their parents, their siblings, their church, their community, and the neighborhood in which they spent most of their lives. And *now* they meet new friends, new foes, new distractions, new demons, and new demands. And if they have lived in the shadow of their parents' relationship with God or their parents' standards and values, this new world will quickly reveal the need to develop their own, thus providing a time of uncertainty and insecurity. So what can we do?

As mentioned in Chapter 5, *communicate*. The Internet has made the world accessible in seconds. Visit them, their school, and their workplace often to keep a connection with the values and standards you have instilled in them.

## Inspect What You Expect.

Inspect, but don't be critical. Talk with their counselors, friends, teachers, the new pastor, and classmates to insure that nothing irrational is taking place without your knowledge of it. We deliberately make sure they have a clean, safe dorm and a safe area to live. We should be equally as demanding that the spiritual environment is not hostile and barren.

# SANITY SAYINGS !

*We're fighting a defeated foe,*
*and we're on the winning team*
*in a fixed fight of which the outcome*
*is already determined.*

# 8

## WHO SINNED, THE SON OR HIS PARENTS?

*And his disciples asked him, saying, Master, who did sin,*
*this man, or his parents, that he was born blind?*
John 9:2

Everyone always wants to pin the blame for defects and destruction on someone else. Have you ever been told "You're just like your daddy" or "You're just like your mama" or "You get that rebellion from your daddy's family"? And the blame game goes on. Jesus said in John 9:3, "Neither hath this man sinned, nor his parents." Sometimes no one sinned. It was a bad decision that led to sin. Sometimes persons are overtaken in a fault (Galatians 6:1). But regardless of the symptom that led to the error, only love can cover, restore, and redeem (I Peter 4:8).

As parents, we must look past our own embarrassment when our kids make some choices that lead to sin. We must reach through our pain and heal them. They don't need any further guilt, condemnation, or accusation from us, but they need our love, our affection, and our understanding. If you really want to damage Satan, who is the real enemy, love your children through every crisis, and they'll grow into powerhouse adults for God.

Don't be used of the enemy to beat them with condemnation. Satan will do plenty of that. Never say, "I'm disappointed in you." Say, "I'm disappointed in your decision." Never say, "I'm ashamed of you." Say, "I'm not ashamed of you, and we and God are going to aid the process of reaching your destiny in spite of these challenges."

Love is the safest environment for producing healthy children who will become healthy adults. Love makes sharing easy. Love makes handling crisis an opportunity for victory instead of the destruction Satan intended. Love makes communication easy. Make sure your children know that you love them. Regularly tell them and show them, and see what a difference love makes.

Affection may be defined as a mental or emotional state or tendency, disposition or feeling, fond or tender feeling, or warm liking. Affection feeds the strength of the personal human spirit and builds habits of normal, healthy intimacy. It constructs channels for wholesome physical touching. These appropriate practices tend to ward off and make repulsive whatever is inappropriate. Lack of affection

fails to build those necessary good practices in one's character.

Adults who lacked affection in childhood many times find it difficult to extend it to their children. Without affection in childhood, adults lack a true working conscience! In a home affection must be shown, and the fruit will remain even when children are adults. A home should provide a place of safety, identity, and grace, where the inhabitants can develop in their intended purpose on the earth. Find ways to affirm, value, esteem, and build up one another. Make the environment of your home an oasis from the destruction, insensitivity, and hostility of a world that chooses to resist God.

Always tell your children, "I love you." There's a difference between saying "I love you" and saying "Love you" or "Love ya" or "We love you." The latter are all generic statements that proceed from our mouth without any connection to our heart. Love that's real has no problem expressing itself. For some fathers, this has to be practiced when saying it to their sons. But you must say, "I love you." The Bible is clear in saying and quoting our God: "For God so loved . . ." you (John 3:16)! And we must do the same.

When love is not communicated from the parents to the children, some wolf will come along and

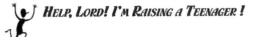 

say it, and before you know it, children are choosing a stranger's stated love over their parents' true love. Children have been with you for fifteen years or more; they should have heard the words "I love you" many times. Train yourself to say "I love you" regularly to your children.

May I remind you that love is patient?

*Charity suffereth long, and is kind;*
*charity envieth not; charity vaunteth not itself,*
*is not puffed up, doth not behave itself unseemly,*
*seeketh not her own, is not easily provoked,*
*thinketh no evil; rejoiceth not in iniquity, but*
*rejoiceth in the truth; beareth all things, believeth*
*all things, hopeth all things, endureth all things.*
I Corinthians 13:4-7

Most of us can love everyone but our own teenagers. I know that some parents are thinking, "You don't know what they have done. That's true. But you know what wrong you've done, and if Christ forgave us of all, we must forgive our teenagers of all and love them unconditionally. We owe everyone love, including our teenagers.

*Owe no man any thing, but to love one another:
for he that loveth another hath fulfilled the law.*
Romans 13:8

## Our Witness Must Start at Home.

*But ye shall receive power, after that the
Holy Ghost is come upon you:
and ye shall be witnesses unto me both in
Jerusalem, and in all Judaea, and in Samaria,
and unto the uttermost part of the earth.*
Acts 1:8

Witnessing, loving, and preaching may appear to have more positive results outside of your immediate family. But there is no joy or personal satisfaction more rewarding than that which is received from the revelation that those that are dearest to your heart are fulfilling purpose and destiny, and you have had a productive part in the victory.

If you have fallen short in this area, a good place to start is with an "I'm sorry" to God first and then to your teenager. Then yield to the very flowing grace of God to give you and your teenager a new start.

## Single Parents, Be Encouraged.

You should not feel the need to be both father and mother; you are one or the other with your original, individual purpose intact (in mind). So don't buy into the lie that you have to be both. Trying to be something or someone that you're not will only lead to frustration and burnout. Remember that whatever you're not is another person's purpose. And God, the God of purpose, will be whatever you need if you'll remain where He told you to be! Walk yielded to your individual purpose. If you have found yourself single again, remember that you are the way you are because of why you are in order to be where He is always. As you remain yielded to God and your individual purpose, God will make His power, grace, and love available to you in unlimited proportion.

*Hear my cry, O God; attend unto my prayer.*
*From the end of the earth will I cry unto thee,*
*when my heart is overwhelmed:*
*lead me to the rock that is higher than I.*
*For thou hast been a shelter for me,*
*and a strong tower from the enemy.*
*I will abide in thy tabernacle for ever:*
*I will trust in the covert of thy wings.*
*Selah.*
Psalm 61:1-4

Don't let how you feel determine your effectiveness or worth as a parent. You too must guard your heart. The enemy of our souls loves to heap condemnation and guilt upon us for how our teenagers have turned out, especially when a marriage never took place or took place and was dissolved. Here is where knowing the voice of God and trusting the sovereignty of God is paramount. Don't live under the cloud of guilt and condemnation. If you keep your heart pointed toward God, all things—and I do mean all things—will work together for you and your teenagers' good.

*Know God, Know Purpose.*
*Know Purpose, Know Passion.*
*Know Passion, Know Power.*
*Know Power, Know Provision.*

*No God, No Purpose.*
*No Purpose, No Passion.*
*No Passion, No Power.*
*No Power, No Provision.*

# *9*

## *Seven Rules of Teen Life*

**Rule #1**     Life is not fair, but God is just.

**Rule #2**     The world won't care about your self-esteem. The world will expect you to accomplish something before you feel good about yourself.

**Rule #3**     You may not make $40,000 per year right out of high school. You may not be a vice president with a car phone, but God will reward faithfulness.

**Rule #4**     If you think your teacher is tough, wait until you get a boss. He doesn't have tenure.

**Rule #5**     Flipping burgers is not beneath your dignity. Your grandparents had a different word for burger flipping; they called it *opportunity!* Vision always sees destiny in opportunity.

**Rule #6**   If you mess up, it's not your parents' fault. They made you; you made the mess. But mercy always makes up for mess-ups. So get up and clean the mess up!

**Rule #7**   Life is not a straight line. It's a circle. You do reap what you sow and face what you left behind until you conquer it.

# *10*

## *ROYALTY IN THE ROUGH*

Yes, they talk strange, look weird, and act like aliens at times. But beneath the veneer of teenage expression, there is a treasure being guarded and garnered for such a time as this. Your teens are the way they are because of why they are. Their purpose is clear in them even if it's not clear to them, and in time they will conform to their purpose and transform into a victorious young adult ready to fulfill the will of God in the earth. You're not alone when you say, "I can't see it." Mary, the mother of Jesus, thought Him strange at the age of twelve.

> And when He was twelve years old, they went up to Jerusalem after the custom of the feast. And when they had fulfilled the days, as they returned, the child Jesus tarried behind in Jerusalem; and Joseph and His mother knew not of it. But they, supposing Him to have been in the company, went a day's journey; and they sought Him among their kinsfolk and acquaintance. And when they found Him not, they turned back again

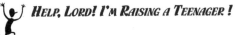 

to Jerusalem, seeking Him. And it came
to pass, that after three days they found
Him in the temple, sitting in the midst of
the doctors, both hearing them, and asking them questions. And all that heard
Him were astonished at His understanding and His answers. And when they
saw Him, they were amazed: and His
mother said unto Him, Son, why hast
Thou thus dealt with us? behold, Thy
father and I have sought Thee sorrow-
ing. And He said unto them, How is it
that ye sought Me? wist ye not that I
must be about My Father's business?
And they understood not the saying
which He spake unto them. And He went
down with them, and came to Nazareth,
and was subject unto them: but His
mother kept all these sayings in her
heart. (Luke 2:42-51)

Jesse thought King David was not even worth pre-
senting to the prophet.

And it came to pass, when they
were come, that he looked on Eliab, and
said, Surely the Lord's anointed *is*

before him. But the LORD said unto
Samuel, Look not on his countenance, or
on the height of his stature; because I
have refused him: for *the LORD seeth*
not as man seeth; for man looketh on the
outward appearance, but the LORD
looketh on the heart. Then Jesse called
Abinadab, and made him pass before
Samuel. And he said, Neither hath the
LORD chosen this. Then Jesse made
Shammah to pass by. And he said,
Neither hath the LORD chosen this.
Again, Jesse made seven of his sons to
pass before Samuel. And Samuel said
unto Jesse, The LORD hath not chosen
these. And Samuel said unto Jesse, Are
here all *thy* children? And he said, There
remaineth yet the youngest, and, behold,
he keepeth the sheep. And Samuel said
unto Jesse, Send and fetch him: for we
will not sit down till he come hither.
And he sent, and brought him in. Now
he *was* ruddy, *and* withal of a beautiful
countenance, and goodly to look to. And
the LORD said, Arise, anoint him: for
this *is* he. (I Samuel 16:6-12)

Jacob thought Joseph had lost his mind.

> And he told *it* to his father, and to
> his brethren: and his father rebuked him,
> and said unto him, What *is* this dream
> that thou hast dreamed? Shall I and thy
> mother and thy brethren indeed come to
> bow down ourselves to thee to the earth?
> (Genesis 37:10)

So, you're in a great company of parents who were
handling kings in the raw! That's right! You are raising tomorrow's psalmists, presidents, CEOs, and
inventors today! They are powerful, expressive,
mosaic, creative, and indifferent due to where they're
going. Much of what we go through is because of
where we're going to.

Technology, chemistry, medicine, economics,
business, and the real world are changing rapidly.
But our God is never unaware, and He never leaves
the earth without a witness. He has a people in preparation who will meet and exceed every expectation
and who will advance the kingdom of God and
enforce the text of Revelation 11:15:

*E. L. WARREN*

*The kingdoms of this world are become
the kingdoms of our Lord, and of his Christ;
and he shall reign for ever and ever.*

# *A Testimony . . .*
# *E. L. and Ella Warren*

M y wife, Ella, and I have raised three teenagers, whose ages were stair-stepped in birth years and at the time of this writing are seventeen, eighteen, and nineteen. We raised them in a Christian, Bible-based, faith-filled environment, and none of the fore-mentioned anesthetized them from being *teenagers*. We experienced everything with them from A to Z.

We also raised them without the aid of resources such as this book, so each of them has challenged our faith, our parenting skills, and our patience. There have been many tense moments. But all three of them are born again, and with the application of the truths in this resource, we firmly believe that they will fulfill their destiny, become productive adults in the earth, and be shining examples of the power of Christ!

# A MIRACLE OUT OF CRISIS...
## MALESSA WARREN

### The Testimony of Malessa Warren,
### My Eighteen-Year-Old Daughter

Two days after I found out I was pregnant this is what I wrote:

1/09/00

*Everything I have ever done seems like a waste to me now. I sit here and think about what I should have done or what I could have done. But the truth is I didn't do them. And now it's time to move on with the future. Forget about the past and all those mistakes. God has forgiven me, so now I am free to move on. Yes, people may talk and say things behind my back, but there is only one person in this world who can judge anybody: God. He knows each and everyone of us. He knows all of what we do, so we can't hide anything from him.*

*When I first found out that I was pregnant, my eyes streamed with tears. Thousands of thoughts ran through my mind. What are my friends, my parents, my teachers, and my relatives going to say? What are they going to think? What is their reaction going to be? How am I going to finish school? I'll have this baby for the rest of my life. I'll have to take care of it by myself. I have to live for my baby and me now. No one else can take care of me. It's all me. I have to do this alone.*

*All of these thoughts ran throughout my mind. I was hurting inside. I didn't know what I was going to do. I felt alone. I was already alone living in this place by myself. I had no one to talk to, no one to go to, no one to cry with, and no one to help me through this. It hurt me. So there I sat and cried. What the lady was saying was now going in one ear and out the other. She was really just talking to herself. For a whole hour or so I sat there crying, knowing I would be hurting other people, especially my parents. They have done so much for me, and I knew they would be hurt.*

*While my head began to throb, she handed me some papers about abortion and adoption, neither of which I would even think about. She handed me the test, and I just stared at it, hoping it would change. It didn't. The two pink lines were still there after all this time. She handed me a model of a baby at the stage in my pregnancy. I held it in my hands like it was the real thing. I cuddled it, rubbed it, smiled at it, and didn't let it go. She handed me some other papers and told me to read them and to take some time just to think about all of this. She prayed that*

*God would take care of me and hold me and comfort me and forgive me.*

*All the time I sat there and thought I really never thought about what God would say. I may have said sorry in my mind but not much else. He should have been the first person I apologized to and thought about what He would say about me. But I didn't. Tears began to stream down again. There was a puddle in my hand. After she was done, I wiped my eyes for the thousandth time and stood up. I walked slowly out of the room. My head was hurting, and my eyes were sore. I walked to my car and sat down. Tears again. I turned it on and began driving, not really knowing where I was going.*

*I ended up at the grocery store. I got what I needed and went home. At home I sat in the dark crying and thinking. I dialed my boyfriend's number. He could tell something was wrong when I said hello. He asked me what I had done that day. I had told him the day before that I was going to the clinic. So I told him what I did, and he asked me what they said. I said, "I am pregnant." A sigh was all I heard at the other end, and then it was "I knew you were." I don't remember much else of what he said that day. My mind was out of it.*

*All night I sat awake, thinking of everything. I thought about what I would have, names, clothes, school, and going home. In the morning, I had a lot on my mind. The first thing I wanted to do was ask my dad about coming home. I was trying to explain to him that I didn't like it there any longer and just wanted to come home. I asked if he wanted me to save some money by not going to school this semester. He told me that it wasn't a waste of his money and that I should stay and finish the semester at least. So I agreed. He then asked why I wanted to come home. I told him it was just because I was ready. He knew it was something more and kept asking. I talked to him three times within two hours, and he kept asking.*

*Finally, I broke down and told him what it was. He did not act like I thought he would. I did not really know what to expect. I knew they would understand, but they were so comforting. I thought to myself that I have the best parents in the world. We talked about what I was going to do about school and my life. He wanted me to stay and finish the semester and then come home and go to school. He said this baby should not change my life or my dreams. I was just going to have to make some adjustments. So I agreed to try and hang in there and finish this semester out. I knew it would be rough, but I was going to do it for him. I would do anything for my parents. After all they did for me, I let them down.*

*He called me later that night and let me know he told my mom. She didn't take it as hard as we thought she would. She had already had a gut feeling that I was pregnant, and God had already prepared her for this. She got on the phone, and I just cried. I hated to do this to them. She was so comforting that night. Her voice was just gentle, and it soothed my heart. I never heard her sound like that before. The rest of that week I do not remember. It was just a lot of crying and hurting.*

Those were my thoughts after the big day. I was always told that when you veer away from God, the devil could get you. I always believed it too. And when I veered away from Him, I didn't really know it. I was still going to church and praising Him and believing in Him. But that wasn't enough. I was away from His presence, and the devil just slipped right in and began taking over. I didn't think he could get to me, but he did. He came in my life and turned it upside down. He has made some changes in my life, but God can turn those around for the best.

God can come into your life and clean up all the mess and mistakes and make them all good. He has done that for me. He has turned being a teenage mom into a joy. My son is such a miracle. He gives me so much joy. Do not ever lose your praise or worship. I told myself when I went to college that the devil couldn't get me with alcohol or drugs. And he didn't. He knew I was too strong in the Lord for that. But he found another way to get me out of the will of God. After I lost my worship, things began to go downhill. I was in two car accidents. I received two speeding tickets in the same day. And I lost both of my jobs. And then to top it all off, I found out I was pregnant. I thought life couldn't get much worse for me.

It did. I began to feel depressed and down. I missed home and my family and friends. I told myself I couldn't go on with school or my career. I lived for the next trip home or for the day my family and friends would come to visit. With God's help, I made it through those four long months. He got me over the troubled waters, and that's what He will do for you. Whenever you have problems, just take them to him, and He will make everything all right. There's nothing He can not handle.

You may make mistakes or decisions that you think no one will understand. God will always understand. Do not try to fix those mistakes by doing something else stupid. Just ask God what to do. I could have had an abortion or tried to hide it from my parents, but I didn't. That would have made things a lot worse. God was right there all the time helping me through, just like he will do for you.

Always remember that your parents took the time to bring you in the world and raise and love you. They will always be there to love and support you, so let them do just that. My parents handled the pregnancy situation wonderfully. They did not make me feel like I was stupid for getting pregnant or that I had made the biggest mistake of my life. They just loved me and stood by my side. One of the first things my dad told me was that this wasn't a mistake; it was just a bad decision. And that's exactly what it was. My son is no mistake. He is in this world for a purpose. If my parents would have handled the situation differently and told me that it was a mistake and that I was dumb and then disowned me, there's no telling what I would have done. I might have had an abortion or even took my life. But thank God, they didn't. They prayed for me and helped me through it all. And now they have a wonderful grandson who they can't stop loving.

You have to let your children live their lives. You can guide them and let them know what is right, but they have to make their own decisions. They may not always be the right ones, but they will learn from their mistakes. It may seem like mistake after mistake, but there will come a time when they get tired

and will get back on track. Just be there to give them your love and support. The more you hassle them, the longer the problem will persist. So be there to guide them and love them. And always remember to keep them in your prayers.

# HELP, LORD!
# I'M BEING RAISED BY A MINISTER!

*The Unedited Testimony of a PK . . .*
*Valecia Warren (age 19)*

## In the Beginning

It's amazing how we are reproduced by a man and woman that we won't even really know until we are about five- or six-years-old. I mean, we know of them: their scent, face, or voice. But at that point, we don't really know them yet. I would have never guessed in a million years that my father would have turned out to be a minister. Living the life of a preacher's kid, better knows as a PK, is a true adventure that no one could relate to but another PK.

In retrospect, being a PK seemed pretty rudimentary in the beginning. It didn't really consist of too much. We would go to church every Wednesday night and Sunday morning, and that would be the end of that. I had a lot of friends, and we would play, talk, or sleep in church on Wednesday nights. When Sunday came along, that's when I would get really excited simply because that meant children's church. In children's church we would get to go to the park, have a different snack every Sunday, play games, and get to talk to each other without the grown folks telling us to be quiet. This also made church go by so quickly, which was a good thing.

It wasn't until I was about fifteen that I started to get the real taste and feeling of having a father as a minister. I began to see the real picture of how it was going to be. I could only go to children's church for so long before we had to advance to the grown people's church. That's when it all began.

The first rule was the no-dating rule. This took me by total surprise, and I wasn't the least bit under-standing. This meant no hanging out with males, no male company at the house, and no phone calls from males. Basically, the male figure was off limits to us. My father would constantly tell me, seeing that I was the oldest, all the information on why not to date. His famous words were, "There is no need to date because God will send you the right man." I would just sit there and stare at him like, "Yeah right." The next reason for not dating was "it's an emotional roller coaster," and this one he would reiterate. All this seemed kind of crazy to me, seeing that I only looked at dating someone as being called the girl-friend of a really cute guy. Obviously to him there was a tad bit more to it than that.

The second rule was that we were only allowed to listen to Christian music. This was the only music allowed in the house. I would get upset with this one because I like to listen to all kinds of music. He would say that the secular music would get in our spirit and mind and have me doing the things that the lyrics said or represented. I would say to him, and still do, that it doesn't affect me like that. I just listen to it. I like the different beats, rhythms, and some of the lyrics. Don't get me wrong. I love Christian music, but I like to listen to whatever I like. I believe that there are different kinds of music that can have major influences on you and encourage you, and then there is the music that can corrupt your mind. It doesn't matter who you are or what you do. This is just my little philosophy.

The third rule was simply outrageous! We were not allowed to participate in or go to any school dances or proms! He saw it as us having the chance to listen and dance to the secular music. According to him, this was also a way to start and get familiar with dating. I mean we were taught not to date, so why would we go and do such a thing? Right? I really don't care what people think about situations in my life, but when my friends would ask me if I was going to a specific dance—homecoming—I would try to convince my dad to let me go. But there was no way around his rules. Most of the time this would just ruin my school spirit about the dance events. I would get lucky on some occasions, and my father would be out of town. I would try to persuade my mother to let me go. She wasn't too much different from my father. Her answer would be no too. The main reason he doesn't want us to date is that he thinks that it eventually will lead to sex.

Sex was a major issue that we discussed on a regular basis. He explained to me that having sex would be the same thing as giving away what was supposed to be for my husband. Sex was not to be done until you got married. He made a covenant with me when I was thirteen, saying that I would not have sex until I got married and giving me a ring to mark the covenant. There were times when I felt pressured by all the talk about not having sex. I thought, "Why is it such a big deal?" Sex didn't really cross my mind at the age of thirteen. His telling me not to have sex or date made the male figure seem like an alien to me. They were totally off limits.

I don't know about you, but when something is made unknown to me, I want to find out the reason why. I mean I know that my parents know what's best for me, but sometimes you want to discover things in your own way. I wanted to know what was so bad about dating, so I went out in the dating world to find out. I had my first boyfriend when I was about fifteen-years-old. This was done in secret, but parents always find out what you don't want them to.

When I got this boyfriend, I didn't see what the big deal was. Like I said before, I just looked at it as being called the girlfriend of a cute guy. My boyfriend and I wouldn't ever talk about sex or anything of the sort. A kiss was brought up later on down the road, but that wasn't such a big deal to me. Seeing how young I was, this relationship was not a big thing, just ordinary puppy love. It wasn't long before it ended because it didn't mean anything to me. It got crazier when I went to high school the next year; other guys started to ask me to be their girl-friend.

The next boyfriend I had turned into a serious thing. There were real feelings beginning to get involved, and we called ourselves in love with one another. This is when I lost my virginity. As each year went by, I felt guiltier for keeping the truth from my dad. Before I knew it, graduation time came around, and I was going to be leaving to go to college. The night of my graduation my dad surprised me with a new car, and he said this was because I was like new since I hadn't had sex yet. If I had sex, I would be used. After he said that, I knew that I had to tell him, so I did. I have never seen my dad as hurt as he was then. I felt so ashamed of myself. Even though I messed up, he was still there to show me

love and to say that everything would be all right. He forgave me.

## On My Own

Soon came the time for me to leave and go off to college. I was absolutely excited. I planned to go to cosmetology school in St. Louis, Missouri. So in July of 1998, I left for St. Louis. I started out doing well until I started to meet the bold and beautiful St. Louis men. They weren't ashamed to confront a female like the Quincy guys were, and of course, it was hard for me to resist them. So I met one guy, we hooked up, and that was all she wrote. I started to realize that I wasn't under my father's wing anymore and that I was free to do my thing.

So I started staying out late, dating whomever whenever I wanted to, drinking, smoking, and basically doing whatever I chose to do. I felt like the world was mine. It all came to an end when my grandma started to call my dad and tell him what I was doing. So he started to keep a closer eye on me. One day I decided to go out and get my eyebrow pierced. The next day my mother came to visit and saw it. She ran right back and told my dad. They were outraged! My dad thought I had lost my mind and had become demonic, which I hadn't.

That next week he came up to St. Louis, pulled me out of school, and made me move back home. I was so angry that I made sure I acted horribly enough for them to send me back. It didn't happen. Instead, my dad started to punish me the way he did when I was younger: whoopings, groundings, etc. Anger triggered out of me more and more when this started to happen. I just knew that I had to stay away from him, so I came to the conclusion to run away. That next day I did it. First, I went back to St. Louis and stayed with a girlfriend of mine. I was too afraid to go to my family that lived in St. Louis. I could only stay at my girlfriend's house for so long, so I ended up going to Chicago and staying with my aunt and uncle for about a week. They ended up calling my parents, of course, and this caused me to end up right back where I had started . . . Quincy, Illinois.

I told myself that the next time I left home, I was going to do it the right way so that I wouldn't have to come back. That is when I started working and saving money until I turned eighteen. I knew that when I turned eighteen I could leave legally, and no one could stop me. My birthday finally came, and I was off, back to St. Louis. I had arranged to have an apartment, find job, and get back into cosmetology school. I had an apartment with hardly any furniture, food, or dishes. When I went back to school, they said that I would have to pay so much a week to stay enrolled, and I couldn't afford that and my apartment. I had to drop out of school.

This is when I met the man of my dreams, or so I thought. He was very attractive, smart, funny, and he loved me for me. The negative traits that he carried were that he didn't have a car, was twenty-one and still lived at home, had no job, and wasn't saved. That should have been my cue to leave him alone, right? Unfortunately, I was blinded by love. I found myself assisting his transportation needs, letting him use my car (in which he would drive his friends around), buying him things, and allowing him to stay at my apartment. Eventually, I ended up letting him move in. That was a terrible mistake. First of all, it wasn't the will of God for me to be with him in the first place. And that is why disaster was brought forth.

## Appearances of the Devil

In the beginning of the relationship, everything worked out fine, but then he eventually started to change. He became possessive and controlling. He screened my phone calls, didn't want me to go out with my friends, and wanted to always be around me. With me being such an outgoing and outspoken individual, this did not find favor with me at all, and it introduced problems into our relationship. I never in my life had to deal with a man who possessed these kinds of traits. At first, I kind of kept quiet about it, but after so long, I started to get frustrated and wanted to get away from him. So I started to speak my mind about how he had been acting. This did not appease him at all. This made him more of an evil person than he was before. He started to get more out of control with his drinking habit. I would try to get him to attend church with me, but church just wasn't on his agenda. He started to pull me farther and farther away from church and God. I began to get in a lot of debt, and he was one of the main reasons why I was in it. With him not having a job, I found myself most of the time accommodating his financial needs.

He was truly an alcoholic but was in total denial about it. His controlling attitude combined with his drinking problem caused him to put his hands on me. I will never forget the first time that he put his hands on me. We were about to leave his family's house, and of course, he had been drinking heavily that day. I wanted to drive my own car, but he was in the controlling mood. He told me to get in the car because he was driving. When we got in my car, we started to argue about something. I can't remember what it was about. He loved to find something to get mad about after he was drunk. While we

were arguing, I began to speak my mind. He told me to shut up, or he would beat the crap out of me. That is when I really started to tell him off.

He then said that since I wanted to talk tough, he was going to show me that he was serious. He took me in a back alley, behind some vacant houses in a dangerous neighborhood, and told me to get out of my own car! I looked at him as if he had lost his marbles. He said, "You think I'm playing with you?" I still didn't move anywhere. When I didn't move after he kept commanding me to, he took my arm and bit it extremely hard. I mean hard to where it turned blue within the next hour. I started to cry with fear and pain. Then he pulled me out of the car and put me on the ground. He started to tell me how bad he was going to hurt me and got himself all worked up. He took my head and started to rub it on the dirty ground. My hair and clothes were filthy afterward. With all my strength, I forced him off me and started to run.

He spotted my purse on the seat in my car, grabbed it, and shook all of my stuff out of it onto the ground. I started to get really angry. I spotted a brick by a dumpster, grabbed it, and ran toward him with it. I looked up at him, and he was crying! I asked what was wrong, and he started apologizing for putting his hands on me. I asked him, "Why would you treat me like that and then call yourself apologizing?" He kept reiterating that he was stupid for doing it, that he was sorry, and that it would never happen again. I believed him, we hugged, and then we went home, with me driving this time.

That wasn't the last time that I saw the devil come out of him like that. He would be his nice person for a couple of weeks, and then as soon as he got alcohol in his system, he would start to act a fool toward me. Instead of having to go through that every two weeks, I would just stay away from him when he started drinking. It only worked for so long. I would find him coming home drunk, trying to start fights with me.

I wanted out so bad, but I had got myself too deep into it. I had myself convinced that he was going to change for the better. I even found myself trying to change him, which was totally the wrong thing to do. It was just getting worse and worse. He started taking my car without asking me and taking my money when he felt like it. He would no longer just use his hands to threaten me. He used suicide. He would make sure that none of my phones worked because he knew that I would call the police in a New-York minute. And he broke things of mine that were special to me.

I will always remember when he broke the sweet-sixteen necklace that my mother had given me for my sixteenth birthday, and after he did it, it was like he didn't feel any remorse about it. Nine out of ten times he would be drunk, stir up trouble, and then pass out. And in the morning when he got up, he never remembered anything from the night before.

One of the worst moments that I have ever felt is when he wrecked my car. He had asked to borrow my car to pick up his cousin. This was around three in the afternoon. I told him to go and come right back, and of course, I believed that he would do as he said. Hours and hours went by, and I was becoming more worried by the minute. I got so worried that I just eventually fell asleep. When I'm worried, I sleep extremely light, so when he came in about four in the morning, I kind of woke up. I was so worn with fatigue that I didn't have the strength to argue with him. I faintly heard him telling me to wake up because he was dying.

At first, I didn't pay him any attention until he kept nudging me to wake back up because he was dying. When I turned on the lights, I almost gagged. He had cut both of his wrists and was bleeding all over the bed and floor. I was on my way to call the police, but then I stopped. In order for him to do something so drastic as to try to commit suicide, he had to have done something wrong first. So I asked him, "What did you do to my car?" He said nothing. I asked him again. Then, he finally admitted that he had wrecked it.

I ran straight outside to look at it, and I just stood there crying, looking at the enormous dent he had created in the back of my car. I ran back inside, and he had passed out from drinking. I knew because the smell of alcohol was so intense on his breath. At that time, all I felt was hatred toward him. So I decided that I wasn't going to call the police; I was going to let him lie there and die. I lay back down and tried to fall back asleep. It was hard for me to go to sleep with the whole incident on my conscience. So I called his mother, and she told me to just make sure that he kept breathing; she said that he would probably be okay.

I went to work that morning. From work I called on the hour to see if he would answer the phone. He never did. The thought kept crossing my mind that he had died, and in a way, I started to get worried. But I also thought that it might be for the best. Then I thought about it, and I especially didn't want a dead body to be lying in my apartment. I rushed home as soon as I got off work, and unfortunately, he had woken up and was just sitting there looking pitiful and, of course, apologetic.

Every time I left him, I really meant it. I never wanted to see him again. But no one could ever know until they are in the situation themselves. It's like you are in a trap that is filled with temptations coming from every angle. I wanted to call my parents and tell them so badly, but I didn't want them to think that I couldn't take care of myself. I was the one who thought I was so grown and who wanted to be on my own.

They ended up finding out about the relationship anyway. Once, I had called my best friend while we were arguing. She was so worried about me that she didn't know what else to do but call my parents. That was one of the best things that she has ever done for me, but at that time I looked at it as if she was telling my business to my parents, whom I didn't want to get involved. Of course, my mom jumped in her van and came to St. Louis to get me. Her plan was overcome. I ended up right back in St. Louis. It was like I was drawn to him in some freaky kind of way. By this time, I had gotten him arrested about three times. The police were beginning to recognize my face and name, which was very embarrassing to me.

I wanted a change. I needed a change. So I applied at the University of Missouri in St. Louis. I was accepted and had figured it all out. I was going to go to school and work, just enough to keep myself busy and keep him off my mind. I really wanted to get over this guy. Things didn't go quite the way that I planned. I moved into the dorms on campus, and down the street there was a bus stop. So he didn't need a car to get to me. He started to come to visit, and I was falling for his nice-guy act all over again. As soon as I fell for it, he messed up again. He had the audacity to stir up trouble in the parking lot of my dormitory while we were in my car. I had seen and had enough of his mess, and I ended it right then and there. As time went by, he would call to make up over and over again for the way he treated me.

I started to see other guys, which wasn't a good idea. It wasn't the right time to be dating other men. It was too soon, and I was vulnerable, trying to replace the good side of him with the other men. It also kept him on his p's and q's. He was calling me constantly, wondering if I had another boyfriend. I gave up as soon as I realized it wasn't the key to my problem. I was trying to focus in school, which was impossible while having to deal with him bothering me and working. My grades dropped terribly. I didn't think that I was going to pass at all. To my advantage, the Lord was watching over me, and I pulled through with His help.

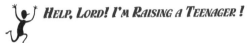 

## The Final Round

Summer finally came, and school was letting out. This meant that I had to move out of the dorms because they were closing for the summer. So I was back to finding another apartment. I wanted to go home in a way, but I still carried the passion of being on my own. My grandmother told me about an apartment that was available across the street from her. I figured that it would be a good idea, seeing that I could help them when they needed it. The only problem was that *he* lived right down the street from the apartment.

Seeing that it had been a long time since we split up, I had a long talk with him to see if he was going to be a hindrance to me staying in the apartment. He said that he would behave himself and that there wouldn't be any problems out of him. Thinking that he could be mature about the whole situation, I moved in. I should have used my head a little bit more while making this decision. On the fourth day of my stay in my new apartment, we went out to a party with our friends. Everything was going just fine. When the party was over, his friends and he decided to go back to his house. So they rode back with me.

When we got in front of my apartment, he said that they wanted to go get some more alcohol. I looked at him and gave him the craziest look, which said, "You must be out of your mind." I simply told him no. He didn't like that at all. So he decided to make me take them by putting my gear in drive and holding his hand on it so I couldn't move it. I said, "Well, we'll just sit here." That's when he threatened that if I didn't drive, he would hurt me. I ended up taking them after that because I didn't have the strength to deal with him anymore. His little acts had become really old to me. Once we got back from getting the alcohol, I was furious. I jumped out of my car and told everyone to get out, and I ran inside my apartment building. I started to get ready for bed and tried to calm myself down. As I was about to get in the bed, I heard a loud boom at my door. I ran to the door and peeked out the window. He had climbed up the building to the second floor, broke through the window, and come to my door.

He was standing there, trying to kick the door down and demanding that I let him in. I had no phone to call the police, and the lady who lived below me was gone. I had no help, but to my advantage God was watching over me. The door started to crack from him kicking so hard. I opened the door and screamed, "What do you want from me?" Immediately, he started pushing me and hitting me. Then he took my head and started to bang it against the walls of my apartment and then on the hard floor. My head began to spin. I started to scream for help and cry with pain. All of the courage that my body had came out of me, and I grabbed him by the skin of his neck and told him to get out if he wanted to live to see another day. I was fed up! He acted as if he was going to leave and then retaliated back at me. He threw me on the bed, grabbed the pillowcase off the pillow, wrapped it around my neck, and began to strangle me. I felt my breath slowly leave my body. I tried to break free, but there was no hope.

All of a sudden thousands of thoughts ran through my head, and I couldn't quite catch on to one. My head was spinning out of control. I slowly opened my eyes, and I didn't know where I was. I started to feel something heavy on my back. My thoughts slowly came back to me, and I figured out where I was. I started to scream at the top of my lungs. I turned around and looked at him with hatred boiling in my eyes and screamed, "You just choked me until I was unconscious!" I could tell by the look in his face that he knew he had and that he thought he had killed me.

I furiously started choking him, spitting in his face, punching him, biting him, and doing everything else you could possibly think of. I told him to get out, and he refused! Then he had the nerve to pass out. I sat there and just stared at him, crying uncontrollably and hating him more and more as each second went by. When I went to the bathroom to get some tissue to wipe my face, I caught a glimpse of my reflection in the mirror. I looked back in the mirror, and I didn't know whom I saw. I had never seen myself so miserable in my entire life as I did at that moment. I just stood there and began to pray. I asked God to help me get my original face back. I wrote an intense journal entry that night.

It was as if God had shown me a sign that it was time to get out of this. This relationship was beginning to mess with me in many ways. At times, I thought I was losing my mind. As I wrote the journal, so many facts that I was once blinded by came to me, and I began to realize that I was a totally different person than I was when I left Quincy. I was finished with being miserable and mistreated by a no-good male. I had been through enough and seen enough to know that it was time for me to change.

## A Sign from God

After that night, I made up my mind that it was time for me to go back home. I tried to tell my parents, but I just couldn't get up the courage to submit to their will. About two nights later, as I was sleeping heavily, the phone rang. I answered it, and it was

my best friend. She sounded so worried, and I started to become anxious to hear what she had to say. She told me that she was just calling me to see if I was okay because she had just had a dream that I had died. I asked her who killed me in the dream, and she said she didn't know. In her dream, she saw herself at my funeral, crying along with many other people. I was so tired that I just said okay and good night. I fell asleep and didn't think anything else of it. About three days later, my mom called to inform me that there was going to be a teen convention at our church that next weekend. She asked me to come and to ask some of my friends if they wanted to come too. I asked around, and one of my friends said that she wanted to go.

The next few days went by fast. He would call and try to come by my apartment building to visit, but I kept my distance because what I had decided was going to stand. It was finally time to go to the convention. The first night of the convention was wonderful. There was a song that was sung that I know God wanted me to hear. The song gave me greater encouragement to be strong with my decision and to keep faith in Him. When church was over, everyone was outside holding different conversations, and a good friend of mine approached me.

She explained to me that she had a dream about me a couple nights back. So I asked her what it was about. She told me that she was hesitant to tell me because it was a horrible dream, and she didn't want me to be scared. I convinced her to tell me anyway. To my surprise, her dream was in accordance with my best friend's dream, and they both had the dreams on the same night. She said that in her dream she was at my funeral, and there were lots of people there crying. I just couldn't believe it. After I really thought about it, I began to get frightened. I automatically knew that the dreams were a sign from God. I figured that the sign was that my life was coming to an end.

I ended up eventually going to my dad, and I told him the scenario and asked him what his thoughts were on the whole situation. He informed me that in the Bible in the book of Genesis it says that when a dream is doubled, it will soon come to pass. I don't think that I have ever been as afraid in my whole life as I was then. I became very careful with everything I ate or drank. I was more careful driving, walking, and being around other people. I began to really freak out about it. After I had worked up the courage, I sat down and explained to my father that I was considering moving back home. He began to get excited and told me that I was always welcome at home.

The convention ended, but I received helpful teachings from it. My friend and I went back to St. Louis. When I got back, things started to go sour. My job at the time was with a temporary agency, and they told me that the job had ended. So I had no job. Then I began to have communication problems with some of my so-called friends. I knew deep down in my heart that it was time for me to go home. I called my dad up and told him that it was finalized; I was coming home. He told me that he and the rest of my family would be up on the Fourth of July, which was two days away, and that they would help me move my things out of the apartment. During those two days, I began to second-guess my decision. I wasn't sure if I was truly ready to go back home and have to deal with rules and regulations. I was so used to being on my own.

During those two days, I ran into my, by this time, ex-boyfriend. I told him that I was moving back home because I just couldn't deal with living there or putting up with him anymore. He tried his best to convince me to stay. I stood my ground and said no. He jumped right into his apologetic mode and started saying that he wouldn't bother me anymore, but this time I was prepared and let none of his words be heard by my ears. I kept telling myself that I had made the right decision and that everything would be all right. Fourth of July came, and my brother packed my personal belongings in my mom's van. I stayed that last night in St. Louis to say good-bye to friends and family. The next day I was on my way home, on my way back to happiness.

## Starting All Over

When I was finally back at home, I thought it was going to be a disaster, but it was actually kind of nice. I had the time now to relax and not be so stressed out about paying bills. I also didn't have to think about the trouble my ex-boyfriend could start. It felt really exhilarating to me. The only minor problem, which wasn't really a problem, was that I was back to having rules enforced on me. After the first week of being home, I began to feel some withdrawal symptoms from the relationship and from St. Louis. I began to yearn for him and eventually started to call him again.

He would still talk about the same things and be the same mean person that he was. Then one day I decided to go to St. Louis with my mother. As we approached St. Louis on the highway, I started to feel sick to my stomach, and when we drove past streets that I knew, I would get the feeling that I wanted to just jump out of the car and stay in St. Louis forever. The feelings were extremely weird. In reality, I

knew that it was only the devil. He was trying to mess with my head and confuse me in any way that he could. I was too strong of a woman to allow that, and God had my back.

As time went by, I began to realize many things. All the things that my dad had taught me in my younger years were all coming true. Everything was beginning to come true about the dating, sex, and other rules he enforced on me. I started to become stronger and resisted making phone calls to my ex-boyfriend, and he began to abandon my thoughts slowly but surely. I started looking for a job back in Quincy. It took me almost two and a half months to find a job. I believe that God planned it that way because I couldn't have asked Him for a better job. I am now employed by United Airlines, and I love it. It is a great career, and I still have fun doing the tasks that it requires.

I remember a sermon that my father once preached. It was about how some people are just so miserable with their jobs that they dread going to work every day simply because they are out of the will of God. I'm not saying that I am totally in the will of God, but God is doing many things in my life. I am working to become more and more close with God each day. All of the debt that I got myself in while I lived in St. Louis is halfway eliminated by the

grace of God. My father and mother, who are greatly blessed with patience, eventually had my car repaired.

I have finally come up with a conclusion about the dreams that were shown to my friends. God showed the dreams to them because I was in total denial about the whole relationship. This was the best way that He could get through to me to help me realize that if I was to stay in that relationship any longer, I would soon be a dead woman. I thank God every night for speaking to my friends through their dreams and letting me know before it was too late. Now I have the opportunity to minister to other people about the troubles that I went through and tell them how they can prevent similar things from happening with the help of God. It feels good to proclaim that I am saved, single, and alive.

# RESOURCES FROM
# E. L. WARREN MINISTRIES INTERNATIONAL

| Title | Series |
|---|---|
| Unmasking Satan | 6 tapes |
| Communication | 6 tapes |
| Power of Purpose | 3 tapes |
| Three-Fold Dimension of Purpose | 2 tapes |
| Is There a Father in the House? | 6 tapes |
| The Family | 8 tapes |
| Well But Not Whole | 4 tapes |
| The Plumb Line Marriage | 4 tapes |

Please visit our Web site at
www.cow-elw.com.

To order from New Dimensions Bookstore, call us
at 1-217-223-3344, ext. 17, or 1-800-453-6712, ext. 17.
We can take only credit card orders over the phone.

You can email us at bishopelw@yahoo.com.

# RECOMMENDED READING

*Making Your Marriage and Life Marvelous*
by E. L. Warren

*Healing: A Different Perspective*
by E. L. Warren

*Positioning Your Faith to Pray the Will of God*
by E. L. Warren

*Pursuit of Purpose*
by Myles Munroe, Ph.D.

*The 21 Irrefutable Laws of Leadership*
by John Maxwell

*Failing Forward*
by John Maxwell

*The Millionaire Mind*
by Thomas J. Stanley, Ph.D.

The Holy Bible

# INTERNATIONAL NETWORK OF AFFILIATE MINISTRIES

*Ministries Touching Ministries to Reach the World*

The International Network of Affiliate Ministries (INAM) is the result of God speaking to the heart of myself and pastors and ministers across the nation and the world who have vision but need a place of covering, fellowship, and accountability. My desire is to introduce INAM and identify those ministries that God desires to be a part.

## Our Vision

To serve pastors, ministers, evangelists, and other servants of the Lord, providing training, resources, and information to identify and fortify the vision that is in their heart and to assist them in its complete and continuous manifestation.

## What Can We Do?

Provide a place of accountability. Assist in the licensing and ordination of ministers. Provide presbytery covering and insight in ministry organization. Provide assistance in incorporation, tax matters, and counseling matters with staff and parishioners (goal setting and disciplining). Train ministers through the Institute of Victory Correspondence Course. Provide support staff and leadership training.

INAM is a vehicle to foster relationships with other ministries nationally and internationally, providing a venue for conferences annually and bringing ministries from around the world together to confer with God and fellowship with one another. INAM is not a denomination and, therefore, does not request an annual report from the affiliate ministries. INAM is not in any way designed to represent an exclusive relationship that prohibits association with other denominations or ministry affiliations.

# ABOUT THE AUTHOR

E. L. Warren is founder and president of E. L. Warren Ministries International, a ministry releasing the revelation put in his heart by the Holy Ghost for the equipping of the Body of Christ.

He has been the senior pastor of The Cathedral of Worship since December of 1980. In 1996, he was ordained and set apart to the five-fold office of apostle to the body of Christ as overseer of INAM (International Network of Affiliate Ministries). In 1998, the International Communion of Charismatic Churches (ICCC) College of Bishops consecrated him for the office of bishop. Archbishop Earl Paulk presided at The Cathedral at Chapel Hill in Atlanta (Decatur), Georgia, and presided at the Installation in Quincy, Illinois, in September of 1999.

E. L Warren has been seen and heard daily on television and radio, and he travels the world, bringing foundation, integrity, and excellence to the Body of Christ in churches, prisons, seminars, conferences, and crusades. He is the author of six books: *Fasting God's Way, Positioning Your Faith to Pray the Will of God, Healing: A Different Perspective, I'm Saved, Now What?, Making Your Marriage and Life Marvelous,* and *Help Lord! I'm Raising a Teenager!* He has also written workbooks for the Institute of Victory, a ministry school of excellence, as well as a manual for new convert training. He is also a writer for *Woman Speaks* magazine.

He has served as a board member of G.M.A.C., an outreach of Oral Roberts University, and on the administrative review board for the Illinois Department of Corrections. He is a former member of Quincy Rotary East and an advisor for Women's Aglow of Quincy. He received the Quincy Jaycee's Top Young Religious Leader's Award in 1983, and has served on the Adams County United Way Board, the Adams County Family Services Board, and the Great Commission Radio Board.

E. L. Warren was born to Eddie and Arleather Warren in Baldwyn, Mississippi. He graduated from St. Louis public elementary and high schools. He also attended the St. Louis University and St. Louis Christian College and graduated from Bailey Technical School. He served as a minister of music at New Northside Missionary Baptist Church from 1970 to 1978. E. L. was born again and filled with the Spirit in 1976. He accepted his call to the ministry in 1978, and was licensed and ordained at New Northside Missionary Baptist Church in 1978 by Reverend Willie Ellis. E. L. Warren has been married since June of 1978, to the former Ella Pearl Rockingham. Their children are Valecia, Malessa, and Roderick. The family currently resides in Quincy, Illinois, where the ministry's corporate headquarters is established.